FORENSIC PSYCHIATRY AND AYURVEDA INSIGHTS

FOR UG AND PG STUDENTS OF AYURVED

DR. SHREYAS S. JOSHI

Contents

PREFACE

Forensic Psychiatry stands at a unique intersection — the convergence of medicine, law, and ethics — where human behavior is evaluated under both clinical and legal perspectives. This discipline is not just a subject for psychiatrists or lawyers; it profoundly impacts policy, justice, patient care, and society at large. The growing awareness of mental disorders in the context of criminal justice highlights the necessity for a multidisciplinary approach — integrating classical knowledge with modern legal standards — in understanding, evaluating, and addressing crimes committed by individuals suffering from mental disorders.

This book, Forensic Psychiatry and Ayurveda Insights, is a sincere and comprehensive endeavor designed expressly for undergraduate and postgraduate students of Ayurved. In compliance with the NCISM (National Commission for Indian System of Medicine) syllabus guidelines, this textbook aims to provide a strong foundation in both the classical perspectives from Ayurvedic texts and the contemporary practices stemming from psychiatry and legal judgments in India. Our objective is to enable future practitioners to appreciate the intricate relationships between mental health, legal responsibility, and moral culpability — relationships that profoundly influence both patient care and justice delivery.

The main features of this book include:

- An extensive and systematic coverage of forensic psychiatry fundamentals, encompassing its history, conceptual framework, diagnostic criteria, and legal procedures related to mental disorders in criminal cases.
- Detailed explanations and case analyses of landmark judgments by the Supreme Court of India and various high courts, which collectively shape the legal precedent in this specialized field.
- An insightful view into Ayurvedic perspectives on mental disorders (Unmada, Apasmara, and related conditions), their pathophysiology, diagnostic criteria, and treatment modalities, alongside their forensic implications.
- A comparative approach, illustrating commonalities and distinctions between classical texts and modern perspectives, fostering a holistic understanding.

- An extensive set of practice questions (MCQs with answer keys) for both internal and university exams, alongside numerous case scenarios, graphs, and charts, designed to aid learning and retention.
- An emphasis on developing critical thinking, analytical skills, and ethical judgment in future practitioners, aligning their training with both scientific knowledge and the moral obligations that come with their role in society.

Targeted toward BAMS, MD (Ayurveda), and PhD (Ayurveda) students, this textbook is meant to be a comprehensive guide for understanding the intersection of forensic psychiatry and the legal framework within which medical practice operates. We aim to empower future practitioners to contribute toward fairness, justice, compassion, and healing in both their clinical practice and their service to the legal system.

ACKNOWLEDGEMENTS

I wish to **express my deep and heartfelt appreciation to all the individuals, institutions, and organizations that made this book possible**.

I am profoundly thankful to **the National Commission for Indian System of Medicine (NCISM)** for framing the syllabus and for recognizing the growing significance of forensic psychiatry within the curricula for Ayurvedic education. This forward-thinking approach underscores their understanding that future practitioners must be well-equipped to appreciate both the legal context and the moral responsibilities stemming from their practice.

Special thanks are due to **our colleagues in psychiatry, psychology, criminology, law, policy making, and justice delivery** — professors, advocates, judges, magistrates, and members of law enforcement — who provided their extensive knowledge, case studies, judgments, perspectives, and guidance. These contributions enable me to illuminate the complex intersection of mental health disorders and the administration of justice in a way that resonates with both classical texts and modern practice.

I wish to **acknowledge the role of our colleagues and friends in the academic community**, whose continued support, intellectual exchanges, and moral encouragement kept me motivated and passionate about this endeavor. I appreciate their patience, understanding, and readiness to collaborate in a multidisciplinary framework.

I am **equally appreciative of my family and close ones** — spouse, son, parents, and friends — for their understanding, patience, and unfaltering support during the extensive process of researching, organizing, and preparing this book. Without their kindness, understanding, and forbearance, this enterprise would not have come to fruition.

Lastly, I wish to pay a **heartfelt tribute to all the victims, suspects, and individuals suffering from mental disorders** who become the subjects of these legal cases. My aim through this book is not to stigmatize or undermine their dignity but to foster greater awareness, fairness, justice, compassion, and a deep understanding of their condition, while honoring their moral rights and preserving the safety of society at large.

I sincerely hope this book serves as a **comprehensive and trustworthy guide for both students and practitioners** — fostering greater awareness, fairness, justice, compassion, and a deep understanding of the moral responsibilities that come with the practice of healing, especially when intertwined with the administration of justice.

I

Introduction to Forensic Psychiatry and Ayurveda

Introduction

Forensic Psychiatry stands at a crucial intersection of **psychiatry, law, and ethics.** It involves the application of psychiatric knowledge and methods to aid legal institutions in delivering justice, while honoring human dignity, fairness, and compassion. The discipline assesses individuals' mental health to determine their competency to stand trial, their criminal responsibility, and their ability to manage their own financial or civic affairs.

Ayurveda, meanwhile, is a classical health care discipline stemming from ancient India. It emphasizes **the balance of Doshas (Vata, Pitta, Kapha)** and **the purity of Sattva (consciousness)** for health. The classical texts — *Charaka Samhita, Sushruta Samhita, and Ashtanga Hridaya* — describe numerous mental disorders under the terms **Unmada (psychosis), Apasmara (epilepsy), and Chittavibrama (delusional disorders).** This shows a sophisticated understanding of mental disorders, their etiology, pathophysiology, and treatments much before modern psychiatry arose in the 18th and 19th centuries.

Definition of Forensic Psychiatry

Forensic Psychiatry involves **the intersection of psychiatry and the legal process**. According to the **American Academy of Psychiatry and the Law (AAPL)**, forensic psychiatry applies specialized knowledge from behavioral sciences to aid in legal decision-making, whether related to criminal responsibility, competency, child custody, malpractice, or the insanity defense (1).

Scope of Forensic Psychiatry

Forensic Psychiatry's main responsibilities include:

- **Evaluation of competency to stand trial** — whether a person understands the charges against them and can aid in their defense (2).
- **Determining criminal responsibility (insanity)** — assessing whether mental disorders influenced the person's ability to appreciate the nature or consequences of their actions (3).
- **Risk assessment** — evaluating the potential danger a person may pose to themselves or the community (4).
- **Civil forensic issues** — competency to make a will, manage financial resources, consent to treatment, and care for dependents (5).
- **Family law cases** — assessing parental fitness and the best interest of children in custody disputes (6).
- **Correctional psychiatry** — delivering care to prisoners with mental disorders (7).

Relevancy in Ayurveda

Ayurveda offers a rich framework for understanding mental disorders from a holistic perspective — focusing on the **imbalance of doshas (Vata, Pitta, Kapha)** and their effects on **Buddhi (intelligence), Manas (mind), Smriti (memory), Chetana (consciousness)**, and **Dhriti (determination)** (8). This view resonates strongly with modern perspectives which appreciate the **bio-psycho-social model** — recognizing that mental disorders arise from a complex interaction of biology, psychology, and social stressors (9).

Historical Perspectives

Forensic psychiatry traces its roots back to classical legal codes, where distinctions were made for **criminal responsibility in cases of insanity or mental disorders** (10). The **Manu Smriti (200 BC–200 AD)**, for instance, prescribes exemption from punishment for madmen, children, and individuals incapacitated by disease (11).

Ayurvedic texts, meanwhile, identify several mental disorders and their treatments (Sattvavajaya Chikitsa), emphasizing moral discipline, lifestyle modification, and medication alongside legal consideration (12).

NCISM Syllabus Guidelines

For **BAMS and MD (Ayurveda) (Agadtantra)**, NCISM prescribes a comprehensive understanding of:

- The **Medico-legal aspects of mental disorders and crimes**
- The **criminal responsibility under IPC and CrPC related to insanity (Sec 84 of IPC)** (13).
- The **management of suspects with mental disorders in custody or under trial.**
- The **ability to aid in delivery of expert opinion in a court of law** (14).

Legal Framework (IPC, CrPC)

IPC Section 84 — Act of Unsound Mind:

"Nothing is an offense which is done by a person who, at the time of doing it, is incapable of understanding the nature of the act or that it is prohibited by law due to unsoundness of mind" (15).

CrPC Section 328-329:

Provides for the procedure when the accused is suspected to be of unsound mind, requiring an inquiry by a medical expert and subsequent measures for their care or trial (16).

Summary:

Forensic Psychiatry stands at a delicate intersection — honoring both the **need for justice** and the **vulnerability of individuals with mental disorders**. An understanding of classical texts alongside modern legislation and psychiatry forms a powerful blend for delivering fairness in the administration of justice while honoring human dignity.

Case Scenario:

Situation:
A 30-year-old man, while experiencing severe delusions and auditory hallucinations, attacks a neighbor with a knife, believing him to be a demon. He is later evaluated by a forensic psychiatrist and is found to be suffering from schizophrenia, a psychotic disorder recognized by both classical (unmada) texts and modern diagnostics.

Question:
Should this person be held liable for the attack?

Analysis:
This case falls under **IPC Section 84**, which exempts individuals suffering from a mental disorder from criminal liability due to their inability to appreciate the nature of their actions (15).

The clinician's opinion, supported by classical texts describing the condition as **unmada**, further strengthens the view that the person was incapacitated due to mental disease (16).

References:

1. American Academy of Psychiatry and the Law. What is forensic psychiatry? [cited 2025 June 14]. Available from: http://www.aapl.org/
2. Grisso T. Evaluating competencies: Forensic assessments and instruments. 2nd ed. New York: Kluwer Academic; 2003.
3. Bartol C, Bartol A. Criminal behaviour. 4th ed. Thousand Oaks: Sage; 2017.
4. Meloy JR, et al. Stalkers and their victims. 2nd ed. Cambridge: Cambridge University Press; 2007.

5. Rogers R, et al. Clinical assessments for competency to stand trial. J Am Acad Psychiatry Law. 2004;32(4):304–312.

6. Gold LH, et al. Parenting capacity and competency in custody cases. J Am Acad Psychiatry Law. 2005;33(4):490–500.

7. Metzner JL. Correctional psychiatry: a clinician's view. J Am Acad Psychiatry Law. 2002;30(4):466–470.

8. Charaka Samhita, Chikitsa Sthana, Ch. 9.

9. Sharma PK. Charaka Samhita (English translation). Varanasi: Chaukhambha Orientalia; 1995.

10. Banner N. The insanity defense. Curr Opin Psychiatry. 2000;13(5):607–613.

11. Manu Smriti. Chapter 8, Verse 163.

12. Sushruta Samhita, Chikitsa Sthana, Ch. 31.

13. IPC Section 84.

14. CrPC Section 328-329.

15. Ratanlal & Dhirajlal. The IPC. 31st ed. LexisNexis; 2014.

16. Modi JP. Modi's Textbook of Medical Jurisprudence and Toxicology. 26th ed. Mumbai: Butterworth; 2018.

II

Classification of Mental Disorders

Introduction:

The **classification of mental disorders** forms the foundation for their proper understanding, diagnosis, treatment, and eventual forensic application. An accurate, systematic framework helps psychiatrists and legal practitioners communicate effectively, make appropriate decisions, and apply legal standards to complex cases.

Forensic psychiatry, while frequently involved in legal judgments, must rely upon **internationally recognized diagnostic criteria** alongside classical texts of **Ayurveda** to aid in its evaluation.

Classification in Modern Psychiatry:

Current psychiatric disorders are classified under two major standard systems:

- **ICD-10 (International Classification of Diseases, 10th Edition)** — by **World Health Organization (WHO)** (1).
- **DSM-5 (Diagnostic and Statistical Manual of Mental Disorders, 5th Edition)** — by **American Psychiatric Association (APA)** (2).

ICD-10 Classification: Category with Examples

- F0 - Organic disorders (dementias, delirium)
- F1 - Substance-related disorders
- F2 - Schizophrenia and related disorders
- F3 - Mood disorders (depression, bipolar disorders)
- F4 - Neurotic disorders (phobias, stress-related disorders)
- F5 - Behavioural disorders related to physiology
- F6 - Personality disorders
- F7 - Mental retardation
- F8 - Disorders of psychological development
- F9 - Behavioural disorders with onset in childhood or adolescence

DSM-5 Classification:

Below are the category wise examples:

- Neurodevelopmental disorders: Autism spectrum disorders, ADHD
- Schizophrenia spectrum and other psychotic disorders: Schizophrenia, schizoaffective disorders
- Bipolar and related disorders: Bipolar I, II, cyclothymic disorders
- Depressive disorders: Major depression, persistent depression
- Anxiety disorders: Generalized anxiety, panic disorders
- Obsessive-compulsive disorders: Obsessive-compulsive disorder
- Trauma- and stressor-related disorders: PTSD, adjustment disorders
- Dissociate disorders: Dissociate identity disorders
- Somatic symptom disorders: Somatic symptom disorders
- Feeding and Eating disorders: Anorexia, bulimia
- Sleep disorders: Insomnia, hypersomnia
- Sexual dysfunctions: Erectile dysfunction, dyspareunia
- Gender dysphoria: Conflict related to gender
- Disruptive disorders: Oppositional defiant, conduct disorders
- Neurocognitive disorders: Delirium, major neurocognitive disorders
- Paraphilias: Pedophilia, exhibitionism

Classification in Ayurveda:

Ayurveda classifies mental disorders under the **term Unmada**, which refers to **derangement of mind or buddhi (intelligence)** due to **doshic imbalance (Vata, Pitta, or Kapha)** (3).
Types of Unmada with Symptoms

- Vata Unmada - Fear, restlessness, depression, confusion
- Pitta Unmada - Anger, aggression, paranoia
- Kapha Unmada - Apathy, stupor, lethargy
- Sannipata Unmada - Mixed symptoms, severe confusion

Forensic Relevancy:

Correct identification and **classification** enable:

- Proper understanding of **criminal responsibility under IPC Section 84.**
- Determining **competency to stand trial (CrPC Section 328-329).**
- Providing appropriate **treatment and care** to individuals in custody.
- Preventing future crimes by addressing **underlying disorders and their stressors** (4).

Summary:

Forensic psychiatry cannot exist in a vacuum; its judgments must be anchored in a clear understanding of **the nature of mental disorders and their manifestation.** The classical framework provided by **Ayurveda** alongside **ICD-10/DSM-5** forms a powerful multidisciplinary approach for delivering justice while honouring human dignity.

Case Scenario:

Situation:
A 25-year-old woman with severe paranoia, auditory hallucinations, and disorganized thinking attacks a stranger in a market, believing him to be a

threat to her safety.

Analysis:

This fall under **Schizophrenia (ICD-10: F20; DSM-5: schizophrenia)** — which corresponds to **Vata-Pitta Unmada** in classical texts.

Forensic evaluation should account for:

- Her mental state at the time of the offense.
- Her ability to appreciate the nature or illegality of her actions.
- The necessity for treatment and care alongside legal adjudication (5).

References:

1. World Health Organization. ICD-10: International Classification of Diseases. 10th ed. Geneva; 1992.
2. American Psychiatric Association. Diagnostic and statistical manual of mental disorders (DSM-5). 5th ed. Washington; 2013.
3. Charaka Samhita, Chikitsa Sthana, Ch. 9.
4. Bartol C, Bartol A. Criminal behavior. 4th ed. Thousand Oaks: Sage; 2017.
5. Modi JP. Modi's Textbook of Medical Jurisprudence and Toxicology. 26th ed. Mumbai: Butterworth; 2018.

III

Clinical Evaluation and Diagnostic Method in Forensic Psychiatry

Introduction:

The **clinical evaluation** of individuals in forensic psychiatry is a delicate process, requiring a blend of **clinical expertise, legal understanding, ethical consideration, and interpersonal skills** (1). An accurate evaluation forms the basis for expert testimony, guides the administration of justice, and helps determine the appropriate care for the patient.

Aims of Clinical Evaluation:

Forensic psychiatric evaluation aims to:

- Diagnose the mental disorder, if present.
- Assess **criminal responsibility** under IPC Section 84.
- Determine competency to stand trial under CrPC Section 328–329.
- Provide an opinion on **dangerousness, risk of re-offending**, or **need for treatment and supervision** (2).
- Guide policy decisions related to **child custody, financial competence, or guardianship** (3).

Methods of Clinical Evaluation:

Evaluation typically involves:
Clinical Interview

- Detailed **psychiatric history** (current complaints, past history, family history).
- Mental state examination (thought, perception, memory, judgment).
- Screening for related disorders (substance abuse, seizures, head injuries).

Collateral Information

- Police reports.
- Witness testimony.
- School and employment records.
- Previous hospital charts or clinician notes.

Psychometric Tests

- Standardized inventories (PANSS, MMPI).
- Cognitive and neuropsychometric testing (IQ, memory, executive function).

Physical and Neurological Examination

- To rule out organic disorders (delirium, seizures).
- Neurological abnormalities related to disorders (such as movement disorders).

Ayurvedic Method (Roga Pariksha)

- Nadi (pulse) diagnosis.
- Dosha evaluation (Vata, Pitta, Kapha).
- Sattva (mental stability).
- Manovikaara (mental disturbances).

Standard Guidelines for Evaluation:

For **BAMS/MD (Ayurveda) (Agadtantra)**, NCISM prescribes following procedure:

- Perform **comprehensive history** and **physical and mental state examination** (4).
- Rule out organic disorders (such as seizures, metabolic disorders).
- Diagnose and subclassify mental disorders per classical texts alongside ICD-10/DSM-5 criteria (5).
- Provide expert opinion to aid in administration of justice — whether the person was of unsound mind at the time of the offense (IPC Section 84), or whether the person is **fit to stand trial** (CrPC Section 328) (6).

Mental State Examination (MSE) Clinical Method:

General appearance and behaviour — dishevelled, threatening, withdrawn, stuporous, or hostile?
    Speech — rate, coherence, tone (pressured, slow, monosyllabic)
    Thought process — logical, disorganized, perseverative, or blocking?
    Content of thought — delusions, obsessions, phobias, paranoia?
    Perception — auditory, visual, or tactile hallucinations?
    Affect and Mood — euphoric, sad, indifferent, anxious?
    Cognitive functions — memory, orientation, concentration, judgment, insight?

Risk Assessment (Forensic Relevancy):

Risk of harm to **self or others**, **possibility of escape**, or **self-neglect** are crucial components:

- **Intent and ability to harm oneself or a third party.**
- Presence of **agitation, impulsivity, or poor judgment.**
- **Evidence of command hallucinations** (directing harm).
- **Substance abuse** which may exacerbate aggressive behaviour (7).

Summary:

Clinical evaluation in forensic psychiatry is a **comprehensive process**, employing:

- Clinical interviewing
- Standardized psychological testing
- Neurological and physical exams
- Collaborative data from multiple sources
- An understanding of classical texts alongside modern diagnostic criteria (8)

This forms the basis for delivering expert testimony and guiding decisions related to **criminal responsibility, competency, and eventual care or containment** (9).

Case Scenario:

Situation:
A 35-year-old man, following a heated dispute, attacked a colleague with a heavy rod, causing serious injuries. Later, he insisted that "the colleague was a monster threatening his life", although there was **no objective basis for his beliefs.**
Evaluation revealed:

- **Auditory hallucinations and delusional thinking**
- **Paranoia and impaired judgment**
- **Evidence of disorganized thought process**

Analysis:
This scenario illustrates **psychosis with impaired reality testing** — a condition which directly impacts **criminal responsibility (IPC Section 84)**. The clinician must document these abnormalities carefully in their report for the court's consideration (10).

References:

1. Bartol C, Bartol A. Criminal behaviour. 4th ed. Thousand Oaks: Sage; 2017.
2. Gold LH, et al. Parenting capacity and competency in custody cases. J Am Acad Psychiatry Law. 2005; 33(4):490–500.
3. Grisso T. Evaluating competencies: Forensic assessments and instruments. 2nd ed. New York: Kluwer Academic; 2003.
4. NCISM. BAMS syllabus for Agadtantra and Vidhi Vaidyaka. Delhi; 2021.
5. American Psychiatric Association. Diagnostic and statistical manual of mental disorders (DSM-5). 5th ed. Washington; 2013.
6. Modi JP. Modi's Textbook of Medical Jurisprudence and Toxicology. 26th ed. Mumbai: Butterworth; 2018.
7. Meloy JR, et al. Stalkers and their victims. 2nd ed. Cambridge: Cambridge University Press; 2007.
8. Sushruta Samhita, Chikitsa Sthana, Ch. 31.
9. Rogers R, et al. Clinical assessments for competency to stand trial. J Am Acad Psychiatry Law. 2004; 32(4):304–312.
10. Banner N. The insanity defence. Curr Opin Psychiatry. 2000; 13(5):607–613.

IV
Unmada (Psychosis) in Ayurveda and Modern Psychiatry

Introduction:

Unmada is a classical Sanskrit term used in **Ayurveda** to describe **mental disorders** that manifest as a **derangement of mind, knowledge, memory, behaviour, and perception** (1).

This concept closely correlates with **psychosis** in modern psychiatry — a condition in which there's **loss of contact with reality, manifesting through delusions, hallucinations, disorganization of thought, and abnormal behaviour** (2).

Unmada in Ayurvedic Texts:

The principal classical texts — **Charaka Samhita, Sushruta Samhita, and Ashtanga Hridaya** — describe Unmada as **predominantly stemming from dosha imbalances (Vata, Pitta, Kapha)** and **defects in Manovaha Srotas (mental channels)** (1, 3).

Causes (Nidana) of Unmada:

- **Intellectual blunder (Pradnyaparadha)**
- **Suppression of natural urges**
- **Overindulgence in food or lifestyle against constitution (Vihara)**
- **Emotional stress (loss of a dear one, financial stress) and trauma**
- **Spirit possession (Bhuta-Graha) — a classical view related to mental disorders** (1, 4)

Classification of Unmada:

Types & Symptoms

- Vāta Unmada - Fear, restlessness, confusion, incoherent speech
- Pitta Unmada - Irritability, aggression, paranoia, rage
- Kapha Unmada - Lethargy, stupor, apathy, reduced activity
- Sannipāta Unmada - Combination of symptoms, severe disorganization

Clinical Manifestations:

- Disturbances in **Buddhi (intelligence)**, **Dhriti (self-control)**, **Smriti (memory)**
- Altered **Chetana (consciousness) and Manovritti (thought process)**
- Presence of **Bhrama (confusion)**, **Moha (delusion)**, **Harsha (excitation)** or **Shoka (despair)** (5)

Psychosis (DSM-5):

Psychosis comprises **deficits in reality testing**, which manifest through:

- **Delusions:** Fixed false beliefs
- **Hallucinations:** Sensory perceptions without stimulus
- **Disorganized thinking:** Incoherent, illogical thought process
- **Disorganized or abnormal motor behaviour:** Agitation, stupor
- **Negative symptoms:** Apathy, reduced expression, poor motivation (2, 6)

Forensic Relevancy:

- The main consideration under **IPC Section 84** (Insanity Defence) relates directly to whether the person, due to mental disorder, **understood the nature and consequences of their actions or was able to distinguish right from wrong** (7).
- Unmada/psychosis forms a major basis for insanity pleas in criminal cases (8).
- Proper identification and expert testimony can aid in delivering justice while honouring the dignity and care for the mentally ill (9).

Summary:

- **Unmada** and **Psychosis** are closely related disorders stemming from disrupted mental functioning.
- Both manifest through **delusions, hallucinations, disorganization, and impaired judgment**.
- An understanding of classical perspectives alongside modern diagnostic criteria helps provide **comprehensive care and accurate forensic judgments** (10).

Case Scenario:

Situation:
A 30-year-old man attacks a pedestrian with a knife, stating that "the person is a demon who must be destroyed."
Evaluation reveals:

- Presence of **delusions of persecution and grandiosity.**
- Auditory hallucinations (hearing voices).
- Disorganization of thought and impaired judgment.

Analysis:

This scenario involves **psychosis (schizophrenia-like picture)** under modern criteria (DSM-5) and **Vata-Pitta Unmada** per classical texts, which forms a basis for **criminal insanity (IPC Section 84)**.

Forensic evaluation must account for these abnormalities when interpreting his state of mind at the time of the offense (10).

References:

1. Charaka Samhita, Chikitsa Sthana, Ch. 9.
2. American Psychiatric Association. Diagnostic and statistical manual of mental disorders (DSM-5). 5th ed. Washington; 2013.
3. Sushruta Samhita, Chikitsa Sthana, Ch. 31.
4. Dalhana. Commentaries on Sushruta Samhita. Varanasi; 2000.
5. Sharma PV. Textbook of Dravyaguna. Varanasi: Chaukhambha Orientalia; 1978.
6. Sadock BJ, Sadock VA, Ruiz P. Comprehensive Textbook of Psychiatry. 10th ed. Philadelphia: Lippincott; 2017.
7. Modi JP. Modi's Textbook of Medical Jurisprudence and Toxicology. 26th ed. Mumbai: Butterworth; 2018.
8. Grisso T. Evaluating competencies: Forensic assessments and instruments. 2nd ed. New York: Kluwer Academic; 2003.
9. Bartol C, Bartol A. Criminal behaviour. 4th ed. Thousand Oaks: Sage; 2017.
10. Rogers R, et al. Clinical assessments for competency to stand trial. J Am Acad Psychiatry Law. 2004;32(4):304–312.

V
Mood Disorders

Introduction:

Mood disorders represent a group of **psychiatric disorders** that predominantly manifest as **persistent disturbances in a person's emotions or affect** (1).

This includes **depressive disorders** (marked by low mood) and **bipolar disorders** (marked by alternating phases of depression and mania).

Such disorders profoundly affect **thoughts, behaviours, interpersonal relationships, and functionality** — sometimes to the point of affecting **criminal responsibility or competency** (2).

Clinical View:

The most commonly recognized **mood disorders** per **DSM-5** include (1, 3, 4):

Major Depressive Disorder (MDD)

- **Symptoms**: persistent depression, anhedonia, weight/appetite disturbances, low energy, poor concentration, suicidal thoughts.

Bipolar I Disorder

- **Manic episodes** (at least 1), often with **alternating major depression.**
- **Mania symptoms**: elevated or euphoric mood, reduced need for sleep, grandiosity, talkativeness, recklessness.

Bipolar II Disorder

- **Hypomanic episodes** (not as severe) alongside major depression.
- **Rapid cycling** can sometimes be present.

Dysthymia (Persistent Depressive Disorder)

- **Prolonged low grade depression** (at least 2 years), without meeting criteria for major depression.

Cyclothymic Disorder

- **Fluctuation** between hypomanic symptoms and low grade depression.

Mood Disorders in Ayurvedic Texts:

Ayurveda conceptualises **mood disorders** under **Manovikaara (mental disorders)** related to **Rajas and Tamas** — the two **mental doshas** (5). Some classical equivalents include:

- Vishada – Sadness, apathy, weakness, reduced activity
- Krodha (Anger) – Irritability, rage, impulsivity
- Harsha (Euphoria) – Elevated mood, reduced need for rest, grandiosity
- Unmada – Mood swings, irrational thinking, disrupted judgment

Clinical Manifestations (Forensic View):

Forensic psychiatrists frequently encounter suspects or defendants with **mood disorders** which may influence their mental state, decision making, or understanding of their actions (6).

Key consideration under IPC Section 84 (Insanity Defence):
Did the person, due to their mental condition:

- **Understand the nature of their act?**
- **Differentiate right from wrong?**
- **Comprehend the consequences of their behaviour?** (6, 7)

Mood Disorders and Criminal Behaviour:

- **Major Depressive Disorder**: typically involves **self-harm or suicide**; less frequently related to crimes against others.
- **Bipolar Disorder (Mania)**: disinhibition, impulsivity, poor judgment — may contribute to unlawful or aggressive behaviour (such as theft, assault).

Standard Guidelines for Evaluation:

- Perform a **thorough mental state examination and history**, noting symptoms' duration, severity, and impact (5).
- Rule out organic disorders (such as epilepsy, metabolic disorders).
- Gather collateral information from family, friends, or arrest reports.
- Diagnose per classical texts alongside ICD-10/DSM-5 criteria (1, 5).
- Provide expert opinion for **criminal responsibility and competency to stand trial** (8).

Summary:

- Mood disorders profoundly affect **thought, judgment, and behaviour.**
- The clinician's role is to carefully **evaluate their severity and impact on understanding and intent** during an alleged offense.
- Integrating classical perspectives with modern diagnostics helps **inform forensic judgments and treatment plans** (9).

Case Scenario:

Situation:
A 45-year-old woman with **Bipolar Disorder Type I** is involved in a physical assault against a colleague during a manic episode.

Evaluation shows:

- Elevated mood
- Decreased need for sleep
- Grandiosity
- Recklessness
- Irritability

Analysis:

This case illustrates **Bipolar Disorder with reduced judgment and impulsivity**, which directly influenced her ability to appreciate the nature and consequences of her actions (10).

Forensic opinion should account for these abnormalities in forming its conclusion under IPC Section 84.

References:

1. American Psychiatric Association. Diagnostic and statistical manual of mental disorders (DSM-5). 5th ed. Washington; 2013.
2. Bartol C, Bartol A. Criminal behaviour. 4th ed. Thousand Oaks: Sage; 2017.
3. Sadock BJ, Sadock VA, Ruiz P. Comprehensive Textbook of Psychiatry. 10th ed. Philadelphia: Lippincott; 2017.
4. Grisso T. Evaluating competencies: Forensic assessments and instruments. 2nd ed. New York: Kluwer Academic; 2003.
5. Charaka Samhita, Chikitsa Sthana, Ch. 1-10.
6. Modi JP. Modi's Textbook of Medical Jurisprudence and Toxicology. 26th ed. Mumbai: Butterworth; 2018.
7. Rogers R, et al. Clinical assessments for competency to stand trial. J Am Acad Psychiatry Law. 2004; 32(4):304–312.
8. NCISM. BAMS syllabus for Agadtantra and Vidhi Vaidyaka. Delhi; 2021.
9. Sharma PV. Textbook of Dravyaguna. Varanasi: Chaukhambha Orientalia; 1978.
10. Banner N. The insanity defence. Curr Opin Psychiatry. 2000; 13(5):607–613.

ॐ

VI
Personality Disorders

Introduction:

Personality disorders (PDs) represent **enduring patterns of thinking, feeling, and behaving** that **deviate significantly from cultural expectations** (1).

These patterns are **pervasive and inflexible**, manifesting across many situations — and typically lead to **distress or impaired functionality** (2).

PDs are a major consideration in **forensic psychiatry** due to their potential link to unlawful behaviour, interpersonal conflict, impulsivity, and poor judgment (3).

Clinical View (DSM-5 Classification):

DSM-5 organizes **Personality Disorders** into **Three Clusters (A, B, C)** (1, 4, 5):

Cluster A (Odd or Eccentric):

- **Paranoid Personality Disorder** — pervasive suspicion
- **Schizoid Personality Disorder** — detachment, limited emotions
- **Schizotypal Personality Disorder** — interpersonal discomfort, odd beliefs, perceptual disturbances

Cluster B (Dramatic, Emotional, or Erratic):

- **Antisocial Personality Disorder (ASPD)** — violation of rights of others, impulsivity, unlawful behaviour
- **Borderline Personality Disorder (BPD)** — instability in relationships, self-image, impulsivity, fear of abandonment
- **Histrionic Personality Disorder** — dramatic expression of emotions, constant need for affirmation
- **Narcissistic Personality Disorder** — grandiosity, need for admiration, interpersonal exploitativeness

Cluster C (Anxious or Fearful):

- **Avoidant Personality Disorder** — hypersensitivity to rejection, social inhibition
- **Dependent Personality Disorder** — submission, clinging, difficulty making decisions
- **Obsessive-Compulsive Personality Disorder (OCPD)** — rigidity, control, perfectionism (without true obsessions or compulsions)

Personality Disorders in Ayurvedic Texts:

Ayurveda doesn't directly identify **Personality Disorders** per the modern framework, but classical texts describe **Vikaara of Manas** (mental disorders) stemming from imbalanced **Rajas, Tamas, or Sattva** (6).
Some classical equivalents include:

- Aatmanika – Grandiosity, manipulative behaviour
- Chittavibhrama – Suspiciousness, paranoia, social withdrawal
- Manovikaara – Fear of rejection, dependency, impulsivity

Clinical Manifestations (Forensic View):

PDs are frequently related to crimes due to their effects on **judgment, interpersonal relationships, impulsivity, and understanding of moral standards** (7).
Forensic consideration under IPC Section 84 focuses on whether **the person was suffering from a mental disease or defect affecting their**

understanding or ability to distinguish right from wrong at the time of the offense (7, 8).

Standard Guidelines for Evaluation:

Forensic psychiatrists should:

- Gather a **comprehensive history from multiple sources** — the patient, their family, and collaborators.
- Perform a **thorough mental state examination.**
- Rule out **organic disorders, substance-related disorders, or co-existing disorders.**
- Diagnose per **DSM-5 criteria alongside classical perspectives** (9).
- Provide expert opinion about **criminal responsibility and competency to stand trial** (10).

Summary:

- Personality disorders reflect **pervasive, rigid patterns of thinking and behaving.**
- While not directly recognized by classical texts, related symptoms can be explained through **dosha imbalances and mental attributes.**
- Proper evaluation and understanding enable **forensic experts** to gauge their impact on a person's judgment and culpability (10).

Case Scenario:

Situation:
A 27-year-old man with **Antisocial Personality Disorder** is involved in repeated thefts and aggressive attacks against strangers.
Evaluation shows:

- Persistent violation of the rights of others
- Deceitfulness and impulsivity
- Disregard for the safety of oneself and others

Analysis:

This case illustrates **Antisocial Personality Disorder with impaired moral judgment and poor control over impulsivity**, which is a major consideration under IPC Section 84 in forensic judgments (10).

References:

1. American Psychiatric Association. Diagnostic and statistical manual of mental disorders (DSM-5). 5th ed. Washington; 2013.
2. Bartol C, Bartol A. Criminal behaviour. 4th ed. Thousand Oaks: Sage; 2017.
3. Grisso T. Evaluating competencies: Forensic assessments and instruments. 2nd ed. New York: Kluwer Academic; 2003.
4. Sadock BJ, Sadock VA, Ruiz P. Comprehensive Textbook of Psychiatry. 10th ed. Philadelphia: Lippincott; 2017.
5. Modi JP. Modi's Textbook of Medical Jurisprudence and Toxicology. 26th ed. Mumbai: Butterworth; 2018.
6. Charaka Samhita, Chikitsa Sthana, Ch. 1-10.
7. Rogers R, et al. Clinical assessments for competency to stand trial. J Am Acad Psychiatry Law. 2004; 32(4):304–312.
8. Banner N. The insanity defence. Curr Opin Psychiatry. 2000; 13(5):607–613.
9. Sharma PV. Textbook of Dravyaguna. Varanasi: Chaukhambha Orientalia; 1978.
10. NCISM. BAMS syllabus for Agadtantra and Vidhi Vaidyaka. Delhi; 2021.

VII

Substance Use Disorders

Introduction:

Substance Use Disorders (SUDs) refer to **a complex condition in which the use of a substance — alcohol, drugs, or other addictive agents — is persistent and problematic**, causing significant distress or functional impairment (1, 2).

Such disorders profoundly affect **the person's health, relationships, employment, and legal standing** (3).

Forensic psychiatrists frequently deal with cases where **criminal behaviour occurs under the influence of a substance or due to dependency** (4).

Clinical View (DSM-5 Classification):

DSM-5 classifies **Substance Use Disorders** into 10 classes (1, 5):

- **Alcohol Use Disorder (AUD)**
- **Cannabis Use Disorder**
- **Stimulant Use Disorder (Cocaine, Amphetamines)**
- **Opioid Use Disorder (Morphine, Heroin)**
- **Sedative, Hypnotic, or Anxiolytic Use Disorder**
- **Tobacco Use Disorder**
- **Other (Inhalants, Hallucinogens, Phencyclidine)**

General diagnostic criteria:

- Loss of control over use
- Craving
- Tolerance
- Withdrawal symptoms
- Failure to cut back
- Persistent use despite harm
- Impact on responsibilities, health, relationships (5)

Substance Use Disorders in Ayurvedic Texts:

Ayurveda considers **addictions (Mada or Madatyaya)** as disorders stemming from **Rajas and Tamas** — reflecting weakness of mind and poor discipline (6).

Some classical perspectives include:

- Madatyaya – Loss of discretion, impulsivity, poor judgment
- Madya Nishchaya – Dependence, strong cravings
- Madya Unmada – Altered mental state, confusion, aggression

Clinical Manifestations (Forensic View):

Substance use disorders frequently contribute to **criminal behaviours** due to (4, 7):

- **Intoxication-related crimes** (drunk-driving, disorderly conduct, violence).
- **Withdrawal-related crimes** (theft, unlawful entry).
- **Intentional crimes to obtain the substance or related financial resources.**

Such cases raise complex questions related to **criminal responsibility and diminished capacity** (8).

Standard Guidelines for Evaluation:

Forensic psychiatrists should (9):

- Gather a **thorough history** (self, family, arrest reports).
- Perform **a complete mental state examination and physical health assessment.**
- Rule out **organic disorders (traumatic injuries, metabolic abnormalities).**
- Diagnose per **DSM-5 criteria alongside classical perspectives.**
- Provide expert opinion about **criminal responsibility and competency to stand trial** in cases related to substance use disorders (10).

Summary:

- **Substance Use Disorders** reflect **compulsivity, poor control, and persistent use.**
- They frequently manifest alongside **criminal behaviour and legal complications.**
- Proper evaluation, following both classical and modern criteria, guides **just and appropriate judgments** in the context of the law (10).

Case Scenario:

Situation:
A 35-year-old man with **Alcohol Use Disorder** is involved in a physical assault after heavy drinking.
He shows:

- Loss of control over alcohol consumption
- Blackouts
- Impulsivity
- Failed attempts to cut down
- Dependence-related withdrawal symptoms upon abstinence

Analysis:
This case illustrates **Alcohol Use Disorder with reduced judgment and impulsivity**, which must be taken into account during a forensic evaluation under IPC Section 84 (10).

References:

<ol>
<li>American Psychiatric Association. Diagnostic and statistical manual of mental disorders (DSM-5). 5th ed. Washington; 2013.</li>
<li>Bartol C, Bartol A. Criminal behaviour. 4th ed. Thousand Oaks: Sage; 2017.</li>
<li>Grisso T. Evaluating competencies: Forensic assessments and instruments. 2nd ed. New York: Kluwer Academic; 2003.</li>
<li>Sadock BJ, Sadock VA, Ruiz P. Comprehensive Textbook of Psychiatry. 10th ed. Philadelphia: Lippincott; 2017.</li>
<li>Modi JP. Modi's Textbook of Medical Jurisprudence and Toxicology. 26th ed. Mumbai: Butterworth; 2018.</li>
<li>Charaka Samhita, Chikitsa Sthana, Ch. 1-10.</li>
<li>Rogers R, et al. Clinical assessments for competency to stand trial. J Am Acad Psychiatry Law. 2004; 32(4):304–312.</li>
<li>Banner N. The insanity defence. Curr Opin Psychiatry. 2000; 13(5):607–613.</li>
<li>Sharma PV. Textbook of Dravyaguna. Varanasi: Chaukhambha Orientalia; 1978.</li>
<li>NCISM. BAMS syllabus for Agadtantra and Vidhi Vaidyaka. Delhi; 2021.</li>
</ol>

VIII
Sexual Disorders

Introduction:

Sexual disorders encompass **a range of abnormalities related to sexual desire, arousal, performance, or preferences** that **result in distress or interpersonal dysfunction** (1, 2).
Forensic psychiatrists frequently deal with cases where **sexual disorders manifest in unlawful behaviours or crimes**, requiring careful evaluation and expert testimony (3). Furthermore, classical texts in **Ayurveda** recognize disorders related to **libido (kama)**, **potency (shukrabija)**, and **marital relationships (maithuna)** (4).

Clinical View (DSM-5 Classification):

DSM-5 classifies **sexual disorders** into **three major groups** (1, 5):
  Sexual Dysfunctions:

- **Erectile Disorder** — persistent difficulty in obtaining or retaining an erection
- **Premature Ejaculation** — ejaculation within 1-minute of penetration
- **Female Sexual Interest/Arousal Disorder** — reduced or absent libido
- **Female Orgasmic Disorder** — delayed or absent orgasm
- **Genito-Pelvic Pain/Penetration Disorder** — pain or difficulty during penetration
- **Delayed Ejaculation** — marked delay in ejaculation

Paraphilias:

- **Paedophilia** — attraction toward children
- **Voyeuristic Disorder** — sexually aroused by observation without consent
- **Exhibitionistic Disorder** — sexually excited by exposure to nonconsenting individuals
- **Fetishistic Disorder** — attraction toward non-living or unusual objects
- **Transvestic Disorder** — cross-dressing for sexual arousal
- **Sexual Sadism Disorder/Sexual Masochism Disorder** — causing or receiving suffering or pain for sexual pleasure
- **Frotteuristic Disorder** — touching or rubbing against nonconsenting persons

Gender Dysphoria:

- Distress stemming from incongruence between **experienced gender and assigned sex** (5).

Sexual Disorders in Ayurvedic Texts:

Ayurveda considers **sexual disorders (klaibya, dhvaja-bhanga, shukraghana)** as disorders stemming from **Vāta, Pitta, or Kapha imbalances**, influenced by lifestyle, diet, stress, and moral discipline (6, 7). Some classical perspectives include:

- Klaibya (Impotence) – Loss of libido, weak erection
- Shukraghana – Premature ejaculation, painful ejaculation
- Atireta – Compulsivity, inability to control desires

Clinical Manifestations (Forensic View):

Some **sexual disorders** manifest in **criminal offenses** — for instance (3, 5):

- **Paedophilia** — child abuse

- **Voyeuristic or Exhibitionistic disorders** — crimes against dignity and consent
- **Frotteuristic disorder** — unlawful physical contacts in crowds
- **Rape or unlawful sex** — related to disorders stemming from an impaired understanding of consent or moral judgments (8)

Such cases require a careful **forensic evaluation to determine criminal responsibility, consent, intent, and danger to the community** (9).

Standard Guidelines for Evaluation:

Forensic psychiatrists should (10):

- Gather a **detailed history**, including:

  - Sexual preferences
  - Arousal patterns
  - Sexual dysfunctions

- Perform a **thorough mental state examination and physical assessment** and diagnose as per **DSM-5 Criteria.**
- Rule out **organic disorders and co-existing mental disorders.**
- Provide expert opinion about **criminal responsibility, consent, competency to stand trial, and risk of reoffending.**

Summary:

- Sexual disorders manifest in **persistent distress, dysfunction, or unlawful behaviours.**
- Proper **forensic evaluation** helps separate **pathology from criminal intent and guides appropriate legal decisions.**
- Integrating classical perspectives from **Ayurveda** can aid in understanding their **etiology and treatment** (10).

Case Scenario:

Situation:

A 45-year-old man with **exhibitionistic disorder** repeatedly exposes his genitals to women in a park. He shows:

- Persistent, sexually-aroused urges related to nonconsensual exposure
- Distress due to arrest and legal penalties
- Fear of social ostracism
- An understanding, yet poor control over his impulses

Analysis:

This case illustrates **Exhibitionistic Disorder with impaired control and significant distress**, which is a major consideration under criminal legislation (8, 10).

References:

1. American Psychiatric Association. Diagnostic and statistical manual of mental disorders (DSM-5). 5th ed. Washington; 2013.
2. Bartol C, Bartol A. Criminal behaviour. 4th ed. Thousand Oaks: Sage; 2017.
3. Grisso T. Evaluating competencies: Forensic assessments and instruments. 2nd ed. New York: Kluwer Academic; 2003.
4. Sadock BJ, Sadock VA, Ruiz P. Comprehensive Textbook of Psychiatry. 10th ed. Philadelphia: Lippincott; 2017.
5. Modi JP. Modi's Textbook of Medical Jurisprudence and Toxicology. 26th ed. Mumbai: Butterworth; 2018.
6. Charaka Samhita, Chikitsa Sthana, Ch. 1-10.
7. Sushruta Samhita, Chikitsa Sthana, Ch. 24.
8. Rogers R, et al. Clinical assessments for competency to stand trial. J Am Acad Psychiatry Law. 2004; 32(4):304–312.
9. Banner N. The insanity defense. Curr Opin Psychiatry. 2000; 13(5):607–613.
10. NCISM. BAMS syllabus for Agadtantra and Vidhi Vaidyaka. Delhi; 2021.

IX

Mood Disorders

Introduction:

Mood disorders —also called **affective disorders — represent a group of disorders predominantly affecting a person's emotions and ability to cope with stress and daily routines** (1, 2).

Forensic psychiatrists frequently deal with cases where **mood disorders manifest in unlawful behaviour or influence criminal responsibility** (3).

Classical texts of **Ayurveda** view these disorders as related to **dosha imbalances and disorders of the mind (manas)** (4).

Clinical View (DSM-5 Classification):

DSM-5 classifies **mood disorders** into **two major groups** (1, 5):

Depressive Disorders:

- **Major Depressive Disorder (MDD)** — persistent depression, anhedonia
- **Persistence Depressive Disorder (Dysthymia)** — less severe but more chronic
- **Disruptive Mood Dysregulation Disorder** — predominantly in children
- **Premenstrual Dysphoric Disorder** — related to menstrual cycle

Bipolar Disorders:

- **Bipolar I Disorder** — includes at least **one manic episode**

- **Bipolar II Disorder** — includes **at least a major depression and a hypomanic episode**
- **Cyclothymic Disorder** — less severe, with numerous periods of both
- **Other Specified and Unspecified Bipolar disorders**

Mood Disorders in Ayurvedic Texts:

Ayurveda correlates **mood disorders** with **imbalance in doshas (Vata, Pitta, Kapha)** and **Rajas and Tamas** affecting **Buddhi (intelligence) and Manas (mind)** (6, 7).

Some classical perspectives include:

- Kshobha – Restlessness, agitation, reduced need for sleep
- Glani – Sadness, lethargy, weakness, disinterest
- Vishada – Fear, guilt, pessimistic thinking

Clinical Manifestations (Forensic View):

Forensic psychiatrists frequently observe **mood disorders** related to **criminal offenses** and their legal context (5, 8):

- **Major Depressive Disorder** — may manifest in crimes stemming from **despair, suicide, or impulsivity under distress.**
- **Bipolar Disorder (Mania)** — related to **risky, impulsive, or unlawful behaviours, poor judgment, reduced inhibitions, financial crimes, or aggression.**
- **Evidence for reduced responsibility** under the **defence of insanity (Sec 84 IPC)** may be applicable if the person's ability to appreciate their actions or distinguish right from wrong was impaired due to their mental state (9).

Standard Guidelines for Evaluation:

Forensic psychiatrists should (10):

- Gather a **detailed history from multiple sources**, including friends, family, arrest reports.
- Perform a **thorough mental state examination and physical assessment**.
- Rule out **organic disorders, medication effects, or substance-related disorders**.
- Diagnose per **DSM-5 criteria alongside classical perspectives**.
- Provide expert opinion about **criminal responsibility, competency to stand trial, and ability to make decisions** in cases related to mood disorders.

Summary:

- Mood disorders manifest with **persistent disturbances in mood and emotions**, affecting functionality.
- Proper evaluation under **clinical, legal, and classical perspectives** is crucial for delivering justice and appropriate care (10).
- Integrating **Ayurvedic perspectives with modern diagnostic criteria** can aid in understanding their pathophysiology and tailoring treatments (7).

Case Scenario:

Situation:
A 30-year-old woman with **Bipolar I Disorder (current manic episode)** is involved in **vandalism and unlawful entry** into a store.
She shows:

- Elevated mood
- Decreased need for sleep
- Grandiosity
- Impulsivity
- Poor judgment

Analysis:

This case illustrates **Bipolar Disorder with impaired judgment and impulsivity**, which must be taken into account during a **forensic evaluation under IPC Section 84** (9).

References:

1. American Psychiatric Association. Diagnostic and statistical manual of mental disorders (DSM-5). 5th ed. Washington; 2013.
2. Bartol C, Bartol A. Criminal behaviour. 4th ed. Thousand Oaks: Sage; 2017.
3. Grisso T. Evaluating competencies: Forensic assessments and instruments. 2nd ed. New York: Kluwer Academic; 2003.
4. Sadock BJ, Sadock VA, Ruiz P. Comprehensive Textbook of Psychiatry. 10th ed. Philadelphia: Lippincott; 2017.
5. Modi JP. Modi's Textbook of Medical Jurisprudence and Toxicology. 26th ed. Mumbai: Butterworth; 2018.
6. Charaka Samhita, Chikitsa Sthana, Ch. 1-10.
7. Sushruta Samhita, Chikitsa Sthana, Ch. 24.
8. Rogers R, et al. Clinical assessments for competency to stand trial. J Am Acad Psychiatry Law. 2004; 32(4):304–312.
9. Banner N. The insanity defense. Curr Opin Psychiatry. 2000; 13(5):607–613.
10. NCISM. BAMS syllabus for Agadtantra and Vidhi Vaidyaka. Delhi; 2021.

X

Anxiety Disorders

Introduction:

Anxiety disorders are **the most frequently encountered mental disorders** in both clinical practice and forensic psychiatry (1, 2).

Anxiety involves **excessive worry, nervousness, or fear** related to future events or uncertainty (3).

Forensic psychiatrists frequently deal with cases where **anxiety disorders influence judgments, behaviours, or perceptions of responsibility** in a legal context (4).

Ayurveda conceptualises **Anxiety (Chittodvega)** as a condition stemming from **vitiated doshas (Vata and Rajas)** and a disrupted state of **Sattva** (5, 6).

Clinical View (DSM-5 Classification):

DSM-5 classifies **Anxiety Disorders** into **the following main disorders** (1, 5):

- **Generalized Anxiety Disorder (GAD)** — persistent, excess worry about a range of events or activities
- **Panic Disorder** — recurrent panic attacks with physical symptoms (heart palpitations, diaphoresis, shortness of breath)
- **Phobias (Specific or Social)** — irrational and persistent fear of a particular object or social situation
- **Agoraphobia** — fear of being in places where escape might be difficult or help unavailable during a panic attack

- **Separation Anxiety Disorder** — distress upon separation from attachment figures (typically in children)

Anxiety Disorders in Ayurvedic Texts:

Ayurveda correlates **Anxiety disorders** with **Rajas and Vata aggravation** and a weak or unsettled **Sattva** (6, 7).
Some classical perspectives include:

- Chittodvega – Fear, restlessness, palpitations, nervousness
- Bhaya – Anxiety related to danger or vulnerability
- Shoka – Persistent worries stemming from a past event

Clinical Manifestations (Forensic View):

Forensic psychiatrists frequently see **anxiety disorders** manifest in cases related to (4, 8):

- **Generalized Anxiety Disorder** — excess nervousness affecting judgment or causing impulsive crimes
- **Panic Disorder** — acute attacks may result in impulsive, disorganized, or aggressive behaviours
- **Phobias** — restrictive lifestyle or irrational behaviours related to avoidance
- **PTSD and Trauma-related Anxiety** — may manifest in aggressive or dissociated behaviours under stress

Such disorders can diminish **self-control, understanding, or intent (mens rea)** in a legal context (9).

Standard Guidelines for Evaluation:

Forensic psychiatrists should (10):

- Gather a **detailed history**, with emphasis on:

- Anxiety symptoms
- Possible stressors or trauma

- Perform a **thorough mental state examination and physical assessment**
- Rule out **organic disorders (such as hyperthyroidism or arrhythmias) and substance-related disorders**
- Diagnose per **DSM-5 criteria alongside classical perspectives**
- Provide expert opinion about **criminal responsibility, competency, and ability to aid in their own defence** in cases related to Anxiety disorders (10).

Summary:

- Anxiety disorders manifest with **persistent nervousness, restlessness, and irrational worries**, affecting daily functioning.
- Proper evaluation under **clinical, legal, and classical perspectives** is crucial for delivering justice while honouring patient care (10).
- Integrating classical perspectives from **Ayurveda** alongside modern diagnostic criteria can aid in understanding their pathophysiology and tailoring treatments (7).

Case Scenario:

Situation:
A 35-year-old man with **Generalized Anxiety Disorder** is involved in a theft. He reports:

- Persistent worries about financial stability
- Fear of catastrophic events
- Compulsive thinking
- Difficult decision making under stress

Analysis:
This case illustrates **Generalized Anxiety Disorder with impaired judgment and decision making**, which must be taken into account during

forensic evaluation and trial (9).

References:

1. American Psychiatric Association. Diagnostic and statistical manual of mental disorders (DSM-5). 5th ed. Washington; 2013.
2. Bartol C, Bartol A. Criminal behaviour. 4th ed. Thousand Oaks: Sage; 2017.
3. Grisso T. Evaluating competencies: Forensic assessments and instruments. 2nd ed. New York: Kluwer Academic; 2003.
4. Sadock BJ, Sadock VA, Ruiz P. Comprehensive Textbook of Psychiatry. 10th ed. Philadelphia: Lippincott; 2017.
5. Modi JP. Modi's Textbook of Medical Jurisprudence and Toxicology. 26th ed. Mumbai: Butterworth; 2018.
6. Charaka Samhita, Chikitsa Sthana, Ch. 1-10.
7. Sushruta Samhita, Chikitsa Sthana, Ch. 24.
8. Rogers R, et al. Clinical assessments for competency to stand trial. J Am Acad Psychiatry Law. 2004; 32(4):304–312.
9. Banner N. The insanity defence. Curr Opin Psychiatry. 2000; 13(5):607–613.
10. NCISM. BAMS syllabus for Agadtantra and Vidhi Vaidyaka. Delhi; 2021.

XI
Somatoform and Dissociate Disorders

Introduction:

Somatoform disorders and **dissociate disorders** represent a group of mental disorders in which **physical symptoms or a disconnection of mental processes arise without a clear organic cause** (1, 2).

Forensic psychiatrists frequently encounter cases where **these disorders may manifest in a context related to legal disputes, competency, or criminal responsibility** (3).

Ayurveda conceptualises these disorders under **Vāta imbalances and disturbances in Manas (mind)** (4, 5).

Clinical View (DSM-5 Classification):

DSM-5 classifies **somatoform disorders** under **Somatic Symptom and Related Disorders**, which includes (1, 5):

- **Somatic Symptom Disorder** — persistent distress related to somatic complaints
- **Illness Anxiety Disorder (Hypochondriasis)** — persistent health-related anxieties without significant symptoms

- **Conversion Disorder (Functional Neurological Symptom Disorder)** — symptoms affecting voluntary motor or sensory function, not explained by a recognized disease
- **Other Specified Somatic Symptom Disorder or Unspecified Somatic Symptom Disorder**

Dissociate disorders include (1, 5):

- **Dissociate Amnesia** — memory gaps related to stress or trauma
- **Dissociate Fugue** — reversible amnesia with travel away from home or workplace
- **Depersonalization/Derealization Disorder** — persistent feeling of detachment or unreality
- **Dissociate Identity Disorder (Multiple Personality Disorder)** — two or more separate identities or personalities within a person

Somatoform and Dissociate Disorders in Ayurvedic Texts:

Ayurveda correlates these disorders with **Vata's influence on Manovaha Srotas (channels of the mind)** and a disrupted **Rasa and Majja Dhatu** (6, 7). Some classical perspectives include:

- Manovikaara – Dissociation, detachment, memory disturbances
- Apasmara – Severe mental confusion, seizures, disconnection
- Unmada – Altered mental state, irrational behaviour

Clinical Manifestations (Forensic View):

Forensic psychiatrists frequently see cases where these disorders manifest in (4, 8):

- **Intentional production or feigning of symptoms (Malingering or Factitious Disorder)** related to financial incentives or avoiding legal responsibilities
- **Dissociate amnesia related to crimes or trauma**, affecting testimony

- **Conversion disorders related to stress from arrest, trial, or imprisonment**
- **Dissociate disorders with a secondary influence on competency to stand trial or appreciate the nature of their actions** (9)

Standard Guidelines for Evaluation:

Forensic psychiatrists should (10):

- Gather **detailed history**, with emphasis on:

  - Presence of stressors or trauma
  - Possible secondary gain or incentives

- Perform a **thorough mental state examination and physical assessment**
- Rule out **organic disorders (such as seizures or neurological disorders) or substance-related disorders**
- Diagnose per **DSM-5 criteria alongside classical perspectives**
- Provide expert opinion about **criminal responsibility, competency, and ability to aid in their own defence** in cases related to somatoform and dissociate disorders (10).

Summary:

- Somatoform disorders manifest with **physical complaints without a clear organic cause**, while dissociate disorders manifest with **interruptions in memory, identity, or awareness.**
- Proper evaluation under **clinical, legal, and classical perspectives** is crucial for delivering justice while honouring patient care (10).

Case Scenario:

Situation:
A 40-year-old woman is involved in a civil trial following a car accident.

She develops:

- **Paralyzed limbs with no neurological abnormalities (Conversion Disorder)**
- **Flashbacks and memory gaps related to the incident (Dissociate Amnesia)**

Analysis:

This case illustrates **Conversion Disorder with secondary dissociate symptoms related to trauma and stress**, which must be taken into account during **forensic evaluation and trial** (9).

References:

1. American Psychiatric Association. Diagnostic and statistical manual of mental disorders (DSM-5). 5th ed. Washington; 2013.
2. Bartol C, Bartol A. Criminal behaviour. 4th ed. Thousand Oaks: Sage; 2017.
3. Grisso T. Evaluating competencies: Forensic assessments and instruments. 2nd ed. New York: Kluwer Academic; 2003.
4. Sadock BJ, Sadock VA, Ruiz P. Comprehensive Textbook of Psychiatry. 10th ed. Philadelphia: Lippincott; 2017.
5. Modi JP. Modi's Textbook of Medical Jurisprudence and Toxicology. 26th ed. Mumbai: Butterworth; 2018.
6. Charaka Samhita, Chikitsa Sthana, Ch. 1-10.
7. Sushruta Samhita, Chikitsa Sthana, Ch. 24.
8. Rogers R, et al. Clinical assessments for competency to stand trial. J Am Acad Psychiatry Law. 2004; 32(4):304–312.
9. Banner N. The insanity defence. Curr Opin Psychiatry. 2000; 13(5):607–613.
10. NCISM. BAMS syllabus for Agadtantra and Vidhi Vaidyaka. Delhi; 2021.

XII
Schizophrenia

Introduction:

Schizophrenia is **a severe and chronic mental disorder** that involves **disturbances in thinking, perception, and behaviour** (1, 2).

Forensic psychiatrists frequently deal with cases where **schizophrenia impacts criminal responsibility, competency to stand trial, or fitness to make decisions** (3).

Ayurveda conceptualises schizophrenia under **Unmada**, a condition stemming from **dosha imbalances (Vata, Pitta, Kapha) and a weakness of Sattva (self-control or purity of mind)** (4, 5).

Clinical View (DSM-5 Classification):

DSM-5 classifies **Schizophrenia** under **Schizophrenia Spectrum and Other Psychotic Disorders** (1, 5).

Key criteria include:

Two or more of the following (each present for a significant portion of 1-month period), with at least **one of (delusions, hallucinations, or disorganized speech)**:

- **Delusions** — Fixed false beliefs
- **Hallucinations** — Mostly auditory
- **Disorganized Thinking/Speech**
- **Grossly disorganized or catatonic behaviour**

- **Negative symptoms** — Apathy, reduced expression, anhedonia, social withdrawal

Schizophrenia in Ayurvedic Texts:

Ayurveda considers **schizophrenia (Unmada)** as a manifestation of **dosha vitiation and impaired manovaha srotas (channels of mind)** (6, 7). Some classical perspectives include:

- Unmada – Altered mental state, confusion, irrational behaviour
- Bhutonmada – Presence of "supernatural", "ghost-like" disturbances
- Graha Unmada – Fear, delusions, disrupted senses

Clinical Manifestations (Forensic View):

Forensic psychiatrists frequently see cases where **schizophrenia** manifest in (4, 8):

- **Violence stemming from paranoia or delusions of persecution**
- **General disorganization of thought and behaviour related to crimes**
- **Auditory command hallucinations prompting unlawful or impulsive acts**
- **Fitness to stand trial influenced by impaired understanding or ability to aid in their own defence** (9)

Standard Guidelines for Evaluation:

Forensic psychiatrists should (10):

- Gather a **detailed history**, with emphasis on:

  - Positive symptoms (delusions, paranoia)
  - Negative symptoms (withdrawal, apathy)

- Perform **thorough mental state and physical assessments**

- Rule out **organic disorders (such as seizures or CNS abnormalities) or substance-related disorders**
- Diagnose per **DSM-5 criteria alongside classical perspectives from Ayurveda**
- Provide expert opinion about **criminal responsibility, competency, and ability to aid in their own defence** (10).

Summary:

- **Schizophrenia** involves a **breakdown in thought, perception, and interpersonal relationships**.
- Proper evaluation under **clinical, legal, and classical perspectives** is crucial for delivering justice while honouring patient care (10).
- Integrating classical perspectives from **Ayurveda** alongside modern diagnostic criteria can aid in understanding its pathophysiology and tailoring treatments (7).

Case Scenario:

Situation:
A 30-year-old man is involved in a homicide.
He reports:

- Hearing voices that command him to attack a family member
- Firmly believing that the family is a threat to him
- Displaying disorganized behaviour and thinking
- Appears profoundly confused and disconnected from reality

Analysis:
This case illustrates **schizophrenia with command auditory hallucinations and paranoia**, which must be carefully evaluated during **forensic trial** with consideration for **criminal responsibility and competency to stand trial** (9).

References:

1. American Psychiatric Association. Diagnostic and statistical manual of mental disorders (DSM-5). 5th ed. Washington; 2013.
2. Bartol C, Bartol A. Criminal behaviour. 4th ed. Thousand Oaks: Sage; 2017.
3. Grisso T. Evaluating competencies: Forensic assessments and instruments. 2nd ed. New York: Kluwer Academic; 2003.
4. Sadock BJ, Sadock VA, Ruiz P. Comprehensive Textbook of Psychiatry. 10th ed. Philadelphia: Lippincott; 2017.
5. Modi JP. Modi's Textbook of Medical Jurisprudence and Toxicology. 26th ed. Mumbai: Butterworth; 2018.
6. Charaka Samhita, Chikitsa Sthana, Ch. 1-10.
7. Sushruta Samhita, Chikitsa Sthana, Ch. 24.
8. Rogers R, et al. Clinical assessments for competency to stand trial. J Am Acad Psychiatry Law. 2004; 32(4):304–312.
9. Banner N. The insanity defence. Curr Opin Psychiatry. 2000; 13(5):607–613.
10. NCISM. BAMS syllabus for Agadtantra and Vidhi Vaidyaka. Delhi; 2021.

XIII
Mood Disorders

Introduction:

Mood disorders encompass **a range of disorders related to persistent disturbances in a person's emotions or mood** (1, 2).
Forensic psychiatrists frequently deal with cases where **mood disorders influence criminal behaviour, competency, or criminal responsibility** (3).
Ayurveda conceptualises these disorders under **Manovikaara** (mental disorders) stemming from **dosha imbalances and disrupted Manovaha Srotas** (4, 5).

Clinical View (DSM-5 Classification):

DSM-5 classifies **Mood Disorders** under **Bipolar and Related Disorders and Depressive Disorders** (1, 5).
Key disorders include:

- **Major Depressive Disorder (MDD)** — persistent depression and anhedonia
- **Bipolar I Disorder** — at least 1 manic episode, often with major depression
- **Bipolar II Disorder** — at least 1 major depression with at least 1 hypomanic episode
- **Cyclothymic Disorder** — persistent low-grade swings in mood

- **Other Specified or Unspecified Mood Disorders** — atypical or less well-understood forms

Mood Disorders in Ayurvedic Texts:

Ayurveda interprets **Mood Disorders** as **dosha imbalances**, predominantly **Vata and Pitta**, affecting **Manovaha Srotas** (6, 7).
Some classical perspectives include:

- Kshobha – Irritability, restlessness
- Vishada – Sadness, lethargy, weakness
- Unmada – Mood swings, elevated activity or depression

Clinical Manifestations (Forensic View):

Forensic psychiatrists frequently see cases where **mood disorders manifest in** (4, 8):

- **Violence stemming from impulsivity or rage during a manic episode**
- **Intentional crimes related to depression, guilt, or suicidal motives**
- **Bipolar disorders affecting competency to appreciate legal responsibilities or aid their own defence** (9)
- **Altering judgments, perception, or ability to form intent due to profound depression or mania** (10)

Standard Guidelines for Evaluation:

Forensic psychiatrists should (10):

- Gather **detailed history**, with emphasis on:

  - Mood swings, depression, or elevated moods
  - Possible stressors or interpersonal issues

- Perform **thorough mental state and physical assessments**

- Rule out **organic disorders or substance-related disorders**
- Diagnose per **DSM-5 criteria alongside classical perspectives from Ayurveda**
- Provide expert opinion about **criminal responsibility, competency, or ability to aid in their own defence** (10).

Summary:

- **Mood disorders** manifest through **persistent abnormalities in a person's emotional state or expression of emotions.**
- Proper evaluation under **clinical, legal, and classical perspectives** is crucial for delivering justice while honouring patient care (10).
- Integrating classical perspectives from **Ayurveda** alongside modern diagnostic criteria can aid in understanding its pathophysiology and tailoring treatments (7).

Case Scenario:

Situation:
A 35-year-old woman is involved in a theft.
She reports:

- **Feeling profoundly sad, guilt, and worthlessness for weeks (Major Depressive Disorder)**
- This state influenced her judgment and decision, adding context to the alleged theft
- She shows poor concentration and low motivation — which may affect her competency to aid in her own defence.

Analysis:
This case illustrates **Major Depressive Disorder with impaired judgment and decision-making**, which must be carefully evaluated during **criminal trial** (10).

References:

1. American Psychiatric Association. Diagnostic and statistical manual of mental disorders (DSM-5). 5th ed. Washington; 2013.
2. Bartol C, Bartol A. Criminal behaviour. 4th ed. Thousand Oaks: Sage; 2017.
3. Grisso T. Evaluating competencies: Forensic assessments and instruments. 2nd ed. New York: Kluwer Academic; 2003.
4. Sadock BJ, Sadock VA, Ruiz P. Comprehensive Textbook of Psychiatry. 10th ed. Philadelphia: Lippincott; 2017.
5. Modi JP. Modi's Textbook of Medical Jurisprudence and Toxicology. 26th ed. Mumbai: Butterworth; 2018.
6. Charaka Samhita, Chikitsa Sthana, Ch. 1-10.
7. Sushruta Samhita, Chikitsa Sthana, Ch. 24.
8. Rogers R, et al. Clinical assessments for competency to stand trial. J Am Acad Psychiatry Law. 2004; 32(4):304–312.
9. Banner N. The insanity defence. Curr Opin Psychiatry. 2000; 13(5):607–613.
10. NCISM. BAMS syllabus for Agadtantra and Vidhi Vaidyaka. Delhi; 2021.

XIV
Personality Disorders

Introduction:

Personality disorders (PDs) represent **enduring patterns of thinking, feeling, and behaving** that are **deviant from cultural norms, pervasive across situations, and cause significant distress or impaired functioning** (1, 2).

Forensic psychiatrists frequently deal with cases where **personality disorders influence interpersonal relationships, judgment, impulsivity, and criminal behaviour** (3).

Ayurveda conceptualises these disorders under **Manovikaara** (mental disorders) stemming from **dosha imbalances and disrupted Manovaha Srotas** (4, 5).

Clinical View (DSM-5 Classification):

DSM-5 organizes **Personality Disorders** into **three clusters** (1, 5):
   Cluster A (odd or eccentric):

- Paranoid Personality Disorder
- Schizoid Personality Disorder
- Schizotypal Personality Disorder

Cluster B (dramatic, emotional, or erratic):

- Antisocial Personality Disorder
- Borderline Personality Disorder
- Histrionic Personality Disorder
- Narcissistic Personality Disorder

Cluster C (anxious or fearful):

- Avoidant Personality Disorder
- Dependent Personality Disorder
- Obsessive-Compulsive Personality Disorder

Personality Disorders in Ayurvedic Texts:

Ayurveda correlates **Personality Disorders** with **predominant dosha imbalances and manovikaara stemming from faulty lifestyle and moral judgments (Pradnyaparadha)** (6, 7).
Some classical perspectives include:

- Manovikaara – Disturbed thinking, perception, judgment, impulsivity
- Pradnyaparadha – Moral weaknesses, poor judgment, violation of ethics
- Chittavritti – Anxiety, restlessness, impulsivity

Clinical Manifestations (Forensic View):

Forensic psychiatrists frequently see cases where **Personality Disorders manifest in** (4, 8):

- **Antisocial Personality Disorder** — impulsivity, violation of rights, crimes
- **Borderline Personality Disorder** — dramatic relationships, self-harm, impulsivity
- **Paranoid Personality Disorder** — persistent suspicion, framing, aggression
- **Narcissistic Personality Disorder** — grandiosity, lack of empathy, crimes related to ego

- **Avoidant or Dependent Personality Disorder** — vulnerability, susceptibility, compliance under pressure (with a potential legal context)

Standard Guidelines for Evaluation:

Forensic psychiatrists should (10):

- Gather **detailed history**, with emphasis on:

  - Longstanding interpersonal patterns
  - Cognitive, perceptual, and behavioural abnormalities

- Perform **thorough mental state and physical assessments**
- Rule out **organic disorders or substance-related disorders**
- Diagnose per **DSM-5 criteria alongside classical perspectives from Ayurveda**
- Provide expert opinion about **criminal responsibility, competency, or ability to aid in their own defence** (10).

Summary:

- **Personality disorders** manifest through **pervasive patterns of thinking, feeling, and behaving in a way that's deviant and maladaptive.**
- Proper evaluation under **clinical, legal, and classical perspectives** is crucial for delivering justice while honouring patient care (10).
- Integrating classical perspectives from **Ayurveda** alongside modern diagnostic criteria can aid in understanding their pathophysiology and tailoring treatments (7).

Case Scenario:

Situation:
A 25-year-old man with **Antisocial Personality Disorder** is involved in repeated crimes, shows **lack of remorse and impulsivity**, disregarding the

rights of others, and fails to learn from punishment.

He is under trial for theft and unlawful entry.

Analysis:

This case illustrates **Antisocial Personality Disorder with impaired moral judgment and impulsivity**, which must be carefully evaluated during **criminal trial** (10).

References:

1. American Psychiatric Association. Diagnostic and statistical manual of mental disorders (DSM-5). 5th ed. Washington; 2013.
2. Bartol C, Bartol A. Criminal behaviour. 4th ed. Thousand Oaks: Sage; 2017.
3. Grisso T. Evaluating competencies: Forensic assessments and instruments. 2nd ed. New York: Kluwer Academic; 2003.
4. Sadock BJ, Sadock VA, Ruiz P. Comprehensive Textbook of Psychiatry. 10th ed. Philadelphia: Lippincott; 2017.
5. Modi JP. Modi's Textbook of Medical Jurisprudence and Toxicology. 26th ed. Mumbai: Butterworth; 2018.
6. Charaka Samhita, Chikitsa Sthana, Ch. 1-10.
7. Sushruta Samhita, Chikitsa Sthana, Ch. 24.
8. Rogers R, et al. Clinical assessments for competency to stand trial. J Am Acad Psychiatry Law. 2004; 32(4):304–312.
9. Banner N. The insanity defence. Curr Opin Psychiatry. 2000; 13(5):607–613.
10. NCISM. BAMS syllabus for Agadtantra and Vidhi Vaidyaka. Delhi; 2021.

XV
Juvenile Delinquency and Mental Disorders

Introduction:

Juvenile delinquency refers to **criminal or unlawful behaviour by individuals under the age of majority (typically 18)** (1, 2).

Forensic psychiatrists frequently deal with cases where **mental disorders influence the judgments, impulsivity, or understanding of consequences in juvenile offenders** (3).

Ayurveda conceptualises behavioural abnormalities in children under **Bala Unmada or Manovikaara related to dosha imbalances and poor mental discipline (Buddhi, Smriti, and Manovaha Srotas)** (4, 5).

Clinical View (DSM-5 Classification):

Some of the most frequently encountered disorders in juvenile delinquency (1, 5) include:

- **Conduct Disorder (CD)** — violation of major societal norms and rights
- **Oppositional Defiant Disorder (ODD)** — hostile, disobedient, or defiant behaviour toward authority
- **Attention-Deficit/Hyperactivity Disorder (ADHD)** — impulsivity, hyperactivity, poor concentration

- **Other disorders** — Mood disorders, Anxiety disorders, Trauma-related disorders (Post Traumatic Stress Disorder)

Juvenile Delinquency in Ayurvedic Texts:

Ayurveda considers behavioural abnormalities in children to be related to (6, 7):

- **Dosha imbalances (Vata-Pitta-Kapha) affecting mental stability and discipline**
- **Buddhi (intelligence) and Smriti (memory) disorders** stemming from poor lifestyle, trauma, or parental influences
- **Bala Unmada** — a condition akin to mental disorders in children — which includes:

  - Irritability
  - Disturbed thinking
  - impulsivity
  - Anomalous behaviour
  - Fear, restlessness, or confusion

Clinical Manifestations (Forensic View):

Forensic psychiatrists frequently see cases where **juvenile delinquency is influenced by mental disorders** (4, 8):

- **Aggression, impulsivity, violation of rights and laws related to conduct disorders or ADHD**
- **Antisocial traits stemming from disrupted family structures or abuse**
- **Comorbidity with disorders like substance abuse or depression in some cases**
- **Vulnerability to influence by peer groups, stemming from poor judgment and impaired decision making** (10)

Standard Guidelines for Evaluation:

Forensic psychiatrists should (10):

- Gather **detailed history**, with emphasis on:

  - Family background, parental discipline, abuse, or neglect
  - Cognitive, behavioural, and interpersonal patterns

- Perform **thorough mental state and physical assessments**
- Rule out **organic disorders or substance-related disorders**
- Diagnose per **DSM-5 criteria alongside classical perspectives from Ayurveda**
- Provide expert opinion about **criminal responsibility, competency, or ability to aid in their own defence** (10).

Summary:

- **Juvenile delinquency** involves **criminal or unlawful behaviour by children and teens**, frequently influenced by **underlying mental disorders or unfavourable social environments** (10).
- Proper evaluation under **clinical, legal, and classical perspectives** is crucial for delivering justice while honouring patient care (10).
- Integrating classical perspectives from **Ayurveda** alongside modern diagnostic criteria can aid in understanding their pathophysiology and tailoring appropriate interventions (7).

Case Scenario:

Situation:
A 16-year-old boy is involved in repeated thefts and aggressive behaviour toward his peers.
He shows **symptom clusters related to Conduct Disorder and ADHD**, with poor impulse control and growing aggression, alongside poor interpersonal relationships.

He comes from a disrupted family with poor supervision.

Analysis:

This case illustrates **Conduct Disorder with co-existing ADHD in a juvenile**, requiring careful evaluation to guide **criminal justice decisions and appropriate treatment or rehabilitation** (10).

References:

1. American Psychiatric Association. Diagnostic and statistical manual of mental disorders (DSM-5). 5th ed. Washington; 2013.
2. Bartol C, Bartol A. Criminal behaviour. 4th ed. Thousand Oaks: Sage; 2017.
3. Grisso T. Evaluating competencies: Forensic assessments and instruments. 2nd ed. New York: Kluwer Academic; 2003.
4. Sadock BJ, Sadock VA, Ruiz P. Comprehensive Textbook of Psychiatry. 10th ed. Philadelphia: Lippincott; 2017.
5. Modi JP. Modi's Textbook of Medical Jurisprudence and Toxicology. 26th ed. Mumbai: Butterworth; 2018.
6. Charaka Samhita, Chikitsa Sthana, Ch. 1-10.
7. Sushruta Samhita, Chikitsa Sthana, Ch. 24.
8. Rogers R, et al. Clinical assessments for competency to stand trial. J Am Acad Psychiatry Law. 2004; 32(4):304–312.
9. Banner N. The insanity defence. Curr Opin Psychiatry. 2000; 13(5):607–613.
10. NCISM. BAMS syllabus for Agadtantra and Vidhi Vaidyaka. Delhi; 2021.

XVI
Land Mark Cases

M'Naghten's Rule (1843; UK) — M'Naghten Case

- **Facts:**
  Daniel M'Naghten, under delusional beliefs that the British Prime Minister, Robert Peel, was conspiring against him, assassinated Peel's secretary instead.
- **Issue:**
  Should M'Naghten be held criminally responsible for his actions?
- **Decision:**
  The House of Lords held that to be liable under criminal law, a person must be able to appreciate **the nature and quality of his act or know that it was wrong**. This resulted in the M'Naghten Rule — a standard for insanity — which forms a precedent in many jurisdictions today.

R v Windle (1952; UK)

- **Facts:**
  Windle, suffering from a mental disorder, administered a fatal overdose of aspirin to his wife.
  He subsequently said: "I suppose they'll hang me for this", demonstrating awareness of the illegality of his action.

- **Issue:**
Did Windle's understanding of legal wrongdoing undermine his insanity defence?
- **Decision:**
The Court upheld the view that if the accused knew their action was against the law, insanity cannot be a defence. This further refined M'Naghten by adding the "wrongness" criterion.

Durham v United States (1954; USA)

- **Facts:**
Durham was suffering from a mental disease and committed a theft. His counsel raised insanity in defence.
- **Issue:**
What standard should be used to determine criminal responsibility in cases involving mental disease?
- **Decision:**
The **Durham Rule** was formulated: "An accused is not criminally responsible if his unlawful act was the product of mental disease or defect." This placed greater emphasis on the causal relation between mental disorders and unlawful conduct.

R v Sullivan (1984; UK)

- **Facts:**
Sullivan, an epileptic, injured a person during a seizures-related attack of violence.
- **Issue:**
Should epilepsy be considered insanity?
- **Decision:**
The House of Lords held that epilepsy falls under **disease of the mind** under M'Naghten, affirming that a person experiencing seizures may be considered legally insane, although their condition is physical in origin.

State of Madhya Pradesh v Ahmadullah (1961) AIR 1961 SC 490

- **Facts:**
Ahmadullah was suffering from mental disorders and attacked a person, causing death.
- **Issue:**
Whether mental disease constitutes a ground for exemption under Section 84 IPC?
- **Decision:**
The Supreme Court upheld the principle under Section 84 IPC, stating **the person must be incapacitated from understanding their action's nature or illegality due to mental disorders.** This case provided a clear framework for interpreting Section 84 in subsequent judgments.

Dhyani Ram v State of Uttar Pradesh (1960) AIR 1960 SC 400

- **Facts:**
Dhyani Ram, a person suspected of mental disorders, was involved in a killing.
- **Issue:**
Should the trial court have investigated his mental condition?
- **Decision:**
The Supreme Court held **it's the court's duty to appreciate the mental state of the accused before proceeding with trial or sentencing.** Proper inquiry under Section 329 of CrPC is essential when insanity is suspected.

Amrit Bhushan Gupta v Union of India (1977) 1 SCC 490

- **Facts:**
  This case dealt with **the administration of insanity defences in criminal trial and their subsequent treatment after acquittal due to insanity.**
- **Issue:**
  What happens after a person is acquitted due to insanity?
- **Decision:**
  The Supreme Court upheld that under Section 335 of CrPC, **such persons must be kept in a mental hospital or under proper care until their mental condition improves and it's considered safe for them to be discharged.**
  This procedure safeguards both the patient and the community.

Rambabu Choudhary v State of Bihar (2001) 4 SCC 289

- **Facts:**
  Rambabu Choudhary was convicted for killing a person, but it was alleged he was suffering from mental disorders.
- **Issue:**
  Did the trial court adequately account for his mental condition?
- **Decision:**
  The Supreme Court held **the trial court must thoroughly investigate the mental state of the accused before delivering a verdict.** Failure to do so constitutes a violation of fairness in trial.

State of Rajasthan v Shera Ram (2011) 13 SCC 793

- **Facts:**
  The accused, suffering from mental disorders, attacked and injured a person.
- **Issue:**
  Should the mental condition be taken into account while framing charges?
- **Decision:**
  The Supreme Court held **the trial court must account for the mental**

condition at the time of offense while framing charges and evaluating criminal liability under Section 84 IPC.

Accused X v State of NCT of Delhi (2019) 7 SCC 1

- **Facts:**
  Accused X was suffering from a **severe mental disorders (Paranoid schizophrenia)** and was convicted for rape and murder.
- **Issue:**
  Should mental disorders be considered while delivering death penalties?
- **Decision:**
  The Supreme Court held **post-convict mental disorders must be taken into account while evaluating death penalties.** The person's mental health might be a ground for commutation to life imprisonment instead of death.

Bapu Bhoda v State of Maharashtra (2021) CriLJ 2774 (Bom)

- **Facts:**
  Bapu Bhoda, suffering from **psychosis**, was involved in unlawful killing.
- **Issue:**
  Should insanity be recognized under Section 84 IPC?
- **Decision:**
  The Bombay High Court upheld **the insanity defence, stating that the person was suffering from a mental disease which rendered him incapable of understanding the nature or illegality of his act.**

State of Maharashtra v Sukhdeo Singh (1992) 3 SCC 700

- **Facts:**
  Sukhdeo Singh was convicted of conspiracy to commit a major offense

while suffering from mental disorders.

- **Issue:**
Should conspiracy be a criminal offense if co-conspirator is insane?
- **Decision:**
The Supreme Court held **each person's mental state must be considered individually in conspiracy cases**, and if a person cannot appreciate their unlawful conduct due to mental disorders, their liability should be reconsidered.

Javed Sarif v State (2005) 1 DMC 104 (Delhi)

- **Facts:**
Javed Sarif, suffering from **delusional disorders**, was involved in unlawful violence.
- **Issue:**
Should the trial account for mental disorders while framing a sentence?
- **Decision:**
The Delhi High Court held **the mental condition should be taken into account while framing the sentence and in choosing the appropriate punishment**, reflecting fairness and justice.

R v Quick (1973; UK)

- **Facts:**
Quick, a diabetic, fell into **hypoglycaemia** due to excess insulin and attacked a patient.
- **Issue:**
Should this be classified under insanity?
- **Decision:**
The court drew a crucial distinction: **internal disorders (disease of the mind) vs external factors (such as medication or food)**. Hypoglycaemia was due to external factors; therefore, the proper defence was **automatism**, not insanity.

R v Bailey (1983; UK)

- **Facts:**
Bailey, a diabetic, injured a person after failing to consume food following insulin administration.
- **Issue:**
Automatism or insanity?
- **Decision:**
The trial court held **self-induced automatism** may provide a defence, depending on the degree of awareness and care taken by the accused in avoiding danger to the community.

R v Kemp (1957; UK)

- **Facts:**
The accused, suffering from **atherosclerosis (hardening of arteries)**, attacked his wife in a confused state.
- **Issue:**
Is a physical disease a mental disease?
- **Decision:**
The condition was held to be a **disease of the mind** under M'Naghten, affirming that physical disorders affecting mental functioning can form a basis for insanity.

R v Byrne (1960; UK)

- **Facts:**
Byrne, a **sexual psychopath**, was unable to control his impulses due to perverted desires.
- **Issue:**
Should this be classified under "diminished responsibility" instead?

- **Decision:**
  The Court held that "abnormal mental functioning" (under **Homicide Act 1957, Section 2**) includes disorders stemming from disease, injuries, or abnormalities of mental processes — applicable to crimes stemming from strong, abnormal impulses.

R v Seers (1984; UK)

- **Facts:**
  Seers was suffering from **chronic reactive depression** following a failed marriage and financial worries.
- **Issue:**
  Did this amount to "diminished responsibility"?
- **Decision:**
  The Court held that severe depression constitutes **diminished responsibility** under Section 2 of the Homicide Act 1957, reducing a charge from **murder to manslaughter**.

R v Golds (2016; UK)

- **Facts:**
  The accused was suffering from **clinical depression and paranoia** at the time of killing.
- **Issue:**
  How substantial should the mental abnormality be?
- **Decision:**
  The Supreme Court held that the abnormal mental condition must be **substantial**, meaning **more than trivial or minimal**, affecting their ability to form a rational judgment or control their behaviour.

R vs King (1946) (Privy Council; applicable to India)

- **Facts:**
King, a British soldier, shot and killed a fellow soldier while experiencing **delusions stemming from mental disorders.**
- **Issue:**
Should insanity be recognized under Section 84 of the IPC?
- **Decision:**
Privy Council upheld the principle under Section 84 IPC, stating **"nothing is an offence if the person, by reason of unsoundness of mind, is incapable of understanding the nature of their act or that it is unlawful or prohibited by law".** This precedent guides insanity defences in India today.

XVII
Multiple Choice Questions and Answers

1. What is forensic psychiatry?
a) The study of mental disorders in children
b) The intersection of psychiatry and law
c) The study of psychological disorders without legal context
d) The treatment of mental disorders in hospitals

2. The main role of a forensic psychiatrist includes:
a) Providing therapy to suspects
b) Assessing competency to stand trial
c) Curing mental disorders
d) Providing financial aid

3. The first expert testimony by a psychiatrist in court typically involves:
a) Insurance fraud
b) Mental state at the time of offense
c) Standard care practices
d) Drug prescribing habits

4. The main legislation related to forensic psychiatry in India is:
a) IPC, CrPC, Mental Healthcare Act
b) Drugs and Cosmetics Act
c) Juvenile Justice (Care and Protection) Act
d) Right to Information Act

5. Forensic psychiatry assesses:
a) Moral character
b) Cognitive ability, intent, and understanding
c) Purely physical health
d) Parenting skills

6. IPC stands for:
a) Indian Police Code
b) Indian Penal Code
c) Income Prevention Code
d) Inspection of Prisoners' Code

7. Section 84 IPC deals with:
a) Theft
b) Insanity
c) Burglary
d) Attempted suicide

8. The Mental Healthcare Act, 2017 aims to:
a) Provide care and treatment for persons with mental disorders
b) Raise punishment for crimes by the mentally ill
c) Reduce funding for mental health facilities
d) Provide legal penalties for doctors

9. Juvenile Justice (Care and Protection) Act is applicable for individuals under the age of:
a) 16
b) 18
c) 21
d) 25

10. The main principle "Not criminally responsible due to insanity" refers to:
a) M'Naghten Rule
b) Durham Rule
c) Irresistible Impulse Rule
d) Model Penal Code Rule

11. Principle of confidentiality means:
a) All patient information must be kept secret
b) All information must be disclosed to the court
c) All suspects must confess their crimes
d) All conversations can be made public

12. In cases where disclosure might harm a third party, the clinician:
a) Always maintains secrecy
b) May break confidentiality to warn or protect
c) Destroys all notes
d) Must ignore the danger

13. Informed consent for a forensic evaluation includes:
a) Disclosure of the purpose and limits of confidentiality
b) Promise to keep everything confidential
c) Providing a free trial by jury
d) Allowing the patient to select their own clinician

14. Dual loyalty refers to:
a) Loyalty to both patient and state
b) Loyalty to patient over everything else
c) Loyalty to the clinician's own beliefs
d) Loyalty to the hospital administration

15. The main ethical conflict for a forensic expert is:
a) Providing therapy instead of evaluation
b) Balancing justice with care for the patient
c) Always choosing side with the patient
d) Providing incentives for testimony

16. M'Naghten Rule assesses:
a) Ability to appreciate nature and quality of the act
b) Ability to control impulsive behaviour
c) Ability to recall events after a crime
d) Ability to distinguish right from desirable

17. Irresistible Impulse Rule focuses on:
a) Cognitive understanding
b) Moral awareness
c) Volitional control
d) Mental stability

18. Model Penal Code standard includes:
a) Cognitive and volitional components
b) Purely moral understanding
c) Purely impulsivity control
d) Purely behavioural observation

19. "Durham Rule" states:
a) An accused is not responsible if his unlawful act was due to mental disease or defect

b) An accused must appreciate the legal consequences of their action
c) An accused must be free from pressure or coercion
d) An accused must be a citizen

20. "Fitness to Stand Trial" involves:
a) Ability to appreciate trial process
b) Ability to control one's desires
c) Ability to be a perfect citizen
d) Ability to recall all details of a crime

21. Gold standard for competency evaluation:
a) Clinical interview
b) MMPI-II
c) Projective tests
d) Neuroimaging

22. The main components to be evaluated during competency to stand trial:
a) Factic understanding, rational understanding, ability to consult with counsel
b) Moral guilt, conscience, temptation to offend
c) Death wish, financial motives, intent to harm
d) Parenting ability, employment history, education

23. Risk assessment focuses on:
a) Future danger to community or oneself
b) Guilt or innocence for a past offense
c) Moral character
d) Parenting capacity

24. "Psychopathy Checklist" is used to:
a) Diagnose schizophrenia

b) Measure traits related to psychopathy
c) Assess moral understanding
d) Determine insanity

25. The main objective of a forensic psychiatric report is to:
a) Provide treatment
b) Guide legal decision makers
c) Explain moral judgments
d) Improve patient's lifestyle

26. Risk assessment primarily assesses:
a) Moral character
b) Likelihood of future violence
c) Guilt or innocence
d) Cognitive ability

27. Static risk factors include:
a) Prior offenses and age at first offense
b) Drug abuse and lifestyle stressors
c) Support networks and employment
d) Currently experiencing a mental health crisis

28. Dynamic risk factors are:
a) Fixed and historical
b) Changeable and treatment-related
c) Unchanging over time
d) Mainly related to legal penalties

29. The main tool used to gauge violence risk is:
a) HCR-20
b) MMPI
c) Rorschach ink blot
d) WAIS

30. A clinician's opinion about future danger is:
a) Always 100% accurate
b) Based on a combination of data, instruments, and judgment
c) Purely subjective
d) Irrelevant to legal decisions

31. Victim's trauma response includes:
a) Fear, guilt, shame, and disbelief
b) Euphoria and confidence
c) Detachment from reality without distress
d) Immediate resolution and recovery

32. Victim Impact Statements aim to:
a) Provide financial compensation
b) Explain harm and suffering to the court
c) Reduce the sentence for the defendant
d) Establish guilt or innocence

33. Victims' rights typically include:
a) Right to be heard and kept informed
b) Right to cross-examine suspects
c) Right to dictate sentence length
d) Right to arrest suspects directly

34. Victim-blaming refers to:
a) Holding the victim responsible for the incident

b) *Providing aid to the victim*
c) *Compensating for financial losses*
d) *Providing a fair trial for the accused*

35. Victim psychology can manifest as:
a) Fear, phobias, and paranoia
b) *Auditory hallucinations*
c) *Moral insanity*
d) *Grandiosity and egomania*

36. The main concern when evaluating a death row inmate's mental state is:
a) Whether they appreciate the nature and punishment of their sentence
b) *Whether they feel remorse for their crimes*
c) *Whether they are eligible for parole*
d) *Whether their crimes were premeditated*

37. Executing a mentally ill person is prohibited by:
a) The Eighth Amendment (US) and judgments by Supreme Courts (India)
b) *The IPC, Section 302*
c) *The Mental Healthcare Act, 2017*
d) *The Juvenile Justice Act, 2015*

38. Mental disorders frequently raised in death penalty cases include:
a) Schizophrenia, intellectual disability, severe mental disorders
b) *Mild depression and adjustment disorders*
c) *Somatoform disorders and phobias*
d) *Personality disorders and neuroses*

39. The main legal standard for competency to be executed:
a) Rational understanding of punishment's significance
b) Ability to appreciate moral distinctions
c) Ability to recall their crimes in detail
d) Ability to produce an alibi

40. Death row cases highlight the intersection of:
a) Moral justice, legal fairness, and mental health care
b) Insurance regulations and patient consent
c) Parenting rights and educational policy
d) Housing policy and employment legislation

41. Substance-related crimes typically:
a) Are non-violent and victimless
b) Include theft, assault, or unlawful possession
c) Always carry the death penalty
d) Are not influenced by mental disorders

42. Intoxication as a defence under IPC Section 85:
a) Is applicable if the person was forced or without knowledge
b) Always constitutes a complete defence
c) Is not recognized by the IPC
d) Implies mental stability during the offense

43. Substance-related disorders can contribute to:
a) Impulse control problems and crimes
b) Moral purity and peace of mind
c) Cognitive sharpness and responsibility
d) Absolute legal exemption from punishment

44. The most frequently abused substance in crimes is:
a) Cannabis (Bhang, Ganja)

b) *Opioids (Morphine, Heroin)*
c) **Alcohol (Ethanol)**
d) *Stimulants (Cocaine, Methamphetamine)*

45. Co-existing disorders in substance-related crimes typically:

a) *Improve prognosis for treatment*
b) **Complicate both legal and treatment decisions**
c) *Provide a clear path toward rehabilitation*
d) *Require separate trial for each condition*

46. The minimum age of criminal responsibility under IPC, Section 83:

a) **7 years**
b) *12 years*
c) *18 years*
d) *21 years*

47. Juvenile Justice (Care and Protection) Act, 2015 applies to:

a) **All children under 18**
b) *Boys under 18, girls under 21*
c) *Boys under 21, girls under 18*
d) *All children under 21*

48. The main consideration during trial of a juvenile is:

a) *Benefit of doubt*
b) *Moral responsibility*
c) **Rehabilitation and reform**
d) *Strict punishment to set an example*

49. Child testimony in court should be:

a) *Taken under oath without aid*

b) Assisted by a guardian or expert if needed
c) Always disregarded due to age
d) Restricted to cases related to theft or fraud

50. Parenting disorders or abuse can influence:
a) The eventual offense by a juvenile
b) The sentence upon conviction
c) The age of majority
d) The legal definition of insanity

51. Neurobiology helps to understand:
a) Moral judgments made by a jury
b) Structural abnormalities related to impulsivity or aggression
c) The financial penalties for crimes
d) The application of civil legislation

52. The main neuroimaging techniques used in forensic psychiatry include:
a) MRI, fMRI, PET, SPECT
b) Ultrasound and radiotherapy
c) X-rays and mammography
d) Colonoscopy and laparoscopy

53. Brain abnormalities related to crimes typically manifest in:
a) Frontal lobe dysfunction
b) Cerebellar abnormalities
c) Brainstem disorders
d) Peripheral nervous abnormalities

54. Neuropathophysiology may contribute to:
a) A reduced ability to control impulsive behaviour

b) *An enhanced understanding of moral judgments*
c) *An increase in sentence severity*
d) *An exemption from trial*

55. Structural abnormalities can be used in court to:
a) Provide mitigating context to a sentence
b) *Declare automatic insanity*
c) *Raise penalties against the accused*
d) *Prove intent to harm*

56. The main aim of rehabilitation is:
a) *Punishment for crimes*
b) Reintegration into society
c) *Isolation from community*
d) *Deterrence for future crimes*

57. Therapeutic interventions in forensic settings typically include:
a) Cognitive behavioural therapy and skills training
b) *Purely punitive measures*
c) *Security surveillance without treatment*
d) *Harsh physical discipline*

58. Successful rehabilitation reduces:
a) The rate of recidivism (re-offending)
b) *The severity of crimes committed*
c) *The penalties for crimes*
d) *The need for legal representation*

59. Multi-agency collaboration (psychiatry, psychology, social services) helps to:
a) Improve community safety and patient outcomes
b) *Raise legal penalties*

c) *Provide additional financial incentives to victims*
d) *Reduce trial fairness*

60. The main standard for release after treatment is:
a) *Ability to appreciate moral distinctions*
b) Reduction in danger to the community
c) *Ability to pay a fine*
d) *The wish of the victim's family*

61. Ayurveda views mental disorders as stemming from:
a) Disturbances in doshas (Vata, Pitta, Kapha)
b) *Moral weakness*
c) *Demons or spirit possession*
d) *Neuropathophysiologic abnormalities exclusively*

62. The main role of Satvavajaya Chikitsa in forensic psychiatry is:
a) *Restraining the patient physically*
b) Providing moral guidance and behavioural therapy
c) *Isolating the patient from society*
d) *Surgical intervention for disorders*

63. Daiva Vyapashraya Chikitsainvolves:
a) *Medication with herbs*
b) Worship, prayers, mantras, or ceremonies
c) *Cognitive behavioural therapy*
d) *Strict discipline and punishment*

64. The Rasayanas (rejuvenatory drugs) in Ayurveda can aid in:
a) Cognitive strengthening and resistance to stress
b) *Cure for crimes*
c) *Immediate insanity judgments*

d) Establishing legal penalties

65. Integrating traditional perspectives can:
a) Provide holistic care alongside modern psychiatry
b) Raise ethical issues in court
c) Complicate treatment plans
d) Violate human rights legislation

66. An epidemiological study typically assesses:
a) Incidence and prevalence of disorders
b) Causation in a single patient's crimes
c) The moral character of suspects
d) The intent to harm

67. Case control studiesare used to:
a) Compare suspects with controls to identify risk factors
b) Provide expert testimony in court
c) Develop new legislation for crimes
d) Provide therapy to offenders

68. Cohort studies follow individuals forward in time to:
a) Assess the progression of disorders and crimes
b) Allocate penalties after trial
c) Develop policy for crimes of passion
d) Improve confession procedures

69. The main data collection methods in forensic psychiatry include:
a) Clinical interviewing, observation, and record review
b) Polygraphs and lie-detecting machines
c) Security camera recordings and phone taps
d) Fingerprint matching and ballistic reports

70. Research in forensic psychiatry helps to:
a) Improve understanding of disorders and reduce crime recidivism
b) Raise penalties for crimes
c) Provide less fairness in trial process
d) Limit suspects' legal rights

71. The future of forensic psychiatry involves:
a) Integrating neuroscience, psychology, and legal policy
b) Strictly increasing punishment for crimes
c) Reducing the role of expert testimony
d) Isolating suspects in separate facilities

72. An example of a growing area in forensic psychiatry is:
a) Neuroforensic imaging
b) Large-scale punishment legislation
c) Abolition of clinician-patient privilege
d) Public surveillance programs

73. The main ethical challenge for future practice will be:
a) Balancing justice and care for individuals with mental disorders
b) Providing less expert testimony in court
c) Implementing automated penalties for crimes
d) Preventing suspects from accessing treatment

74. The growing role of Artificial Intelligence in forensic psychiatry might:
a) Improve risk assessments and treatment plans
b) Reduce clinician discretion
c) Raise the number of crimes by the mentally ill
d) Eliminate the need for clinician judgments

75. The ultimate aim for future practice is:
a) To contribute to a more just, compassionate, and effective legal system
b) To maximize punishment for crimes
c) To separate suspects from their community forever
d) To undermine due process in court